My World

Sizes

Ruth Merttens

Heinemann Library
Chicago, Illinois

Customer Service 888-454-2279

Visit our website at www.heinemannlibrary.com

Printed and bound in China by South China Printing Co. Ltd.

09 08 07 06
10 9 8 7 6 5 4 3 2

Library of Congress Cataloging-in-Publication Data
Merttens, Ruth.
  Sizes / Ruth Merttens.
       p. cm. – (My world)
  Includes bibliographical references and index.
  ISBN 1-4034-6463-4 (lib. bdg.) – ISBN 1-4034-6468-5 (pbk.)
  1. Size perception--Juvenile literature. 2. Size judgment--Juvenile literature. I. Title: Sizes. II. Title.
  BF299.S5M47 2005
  153.7'52--dc22

                                          2004016144

Acknowledgments
The publisher would like to thank the following for permission to reproduce photographs:
NHPA/Alan Barnes pp. 20, 21a; NHPA/Ant Photo Library pp. 12, 13a; RSPCA Photolibrary pp. 10, 11a; Tudor Photography pp. 4, 5, 6, 7, 8, 9, 11b, 13b, 14, 15, 16, 17, 18, 19, 21b, 22, 23, 24.

Cover photograph reproduced with permission of Pete Morris.

Every effort has been made to contact copyright holders of any material reproduced in this book. Any omissions will be rectified in subsequent printings if notice is given to the publisher.

Many thanks to the teachers, library media specialists, reading instructors, and educational consultants who have helped develop the Read and Learn/Lee y aprende brand.

Some words are shown in bold, **like this.**
You can find them in the picture glossary on page 24.

Contents

How Tall Are You?

Everyone tells you how tall you are getting.

You can use a **growth chart** to see how tall you are.

You **compare** how tall you are with the lines on the chart.

Comparing is looking at two things together.

Who Is Taller?

This dog is a Great Dane.

A Great Dane is as tall as a yardstick.

Compare the girl to the dog.

The girl is taller than the dog.

Are You Bigger Than a Horse?

This is a bay horse.

Horses are big and strong.

Compare the horse to the boy.

The horse is much bigger.

Are You Bigger Than an Elephant?

This is an African elephant.

Elephants are the biggest land animals in the world.

Compare the girl to the elephant.

This elephant is much bigger than the girl.

Are You Longer Than a Whale?

This is a humpback whale.

A humpback whale is about as long as a school bus.

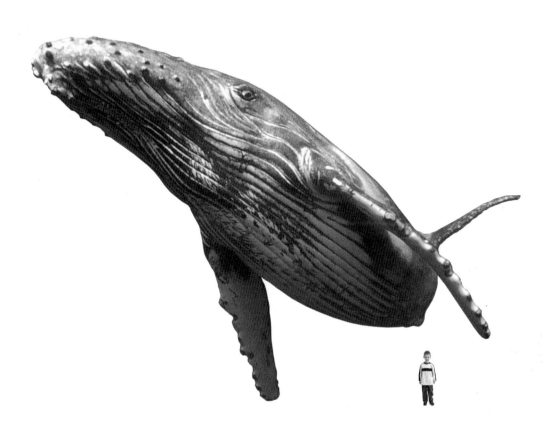

When you lie down, you are as long as a table.

A humpback whale is about ten times as long as you!

Are You Taller Than a Pony?

This is a Shetland pony.

A Shetland pony is about as tall as a yardstick.

Compare the girl to the pony.

The girl is taller than the pony.

Are You Taller Than This Dog?

This is a Yorkshire terrier.

It is about as tall as a cat.

Compare the boy to the dog.

A boy is about four times taller than a Yorkshire terrier.

Are You Taller Than a Cat?

This is a tabby cat.

Most pet cats are about as tall as a big bag of sugar.

Compare the cat to the girl.

The girl is about four times taller than the cat.

Are You Taller Than a Butterfly?

This is a silver-studded blue butterfly.

When it stands, it is about as tall as a small coin.

Compare the butterfly to the boy.

A boy is about 47 times taller than a butterfly!

How Do You Measure Up?

Some animals are really big.

Can you think of some animals that are bigger than you are?

Other animals are really small.

Can you think of some animals that are smaller than you are?

Picture Glossary

compare
pages 5, 7, 9, 11, 15, 19, 21
look at two things together

growth chart
page 4
picture that shows
how tall you are

Index